RENGA *for* OBAMA

AN OCCASIONAL POEM

edited by
MAJOR JACKSON

HARVARD REVIEW **HR** CHAPBOOK *No. 1*

Published by Harvard Review
HOUGHTON LIBRARY
HARVARD UNIVERSITY
CAMBRIDGE, MA 02138
harvardreview.org

First published at Harvard Review Online, January 21, 2017, to April 30, 2017

©2018 by the President and Fellows of Harvard College

All rights reserved

ISBN: 978-0-9652372-1-5

Library of Congress Control Number: 2017957742

Design by Alex Camlin
Printed by The Prolific Group, Canada

CONTENTS

Introduction by Major Jackson • v

RENGA *for* OBAMA • 1

Contributors • 137

Acknowledgments • 148

INTRODUCTION

Renga for Obama was conceived one evening in January 2017 in a spirit of despair and hopeful optimism as a kind of bridge between the two. Like much of the country, I felt the massive divisions the election of 2016 had wrought upon the nation. The news made clear that immigration, terrorism, sexism, and racism, frequently manipulated in election seasons as rhetorical ballast, had seeded fear, distrust, and dissension among Americans. We were, once again, a nation at war with itself.

  What dawned on me that night was the immense symbolism and meaning of Barack Obama's presidency not only for our children and the generation of Americans who did not live long enough to see (and, even more tragically, could never have imagined) a black man in the White House but for all those who believe in the evolution of society toward a better version of itself and in the core democratic values of representative government. This is what we celebrated in 2008, and in the waning days of Barack Obama's presidency, watching the endless newsfeed of national discord, it seemed to me necessary to remember the road we had taken and to commemorate it. Together, as a nation, we had taken a quantum leap forward; we had witnessed something different and special in the progress of our nation toward the goal of forming "a more perfect Union."

That night I wrote a manifesto that spoke to the redemptive power of art and the triumph of righteous ideals that are born from the imagination. It spoke of the importance of tolerance and of our common bonds, how as a society the welfare of the least among us is interwoven with the fate and decisions of the most prosperous, and how we measure the strength of a civilization by the collective regard we have for each other, and how we should not lose sight of the nobility of the office of the president in promoting and advocating such values, which Obama's tenure seemed to epitomize.

In the course of writing this credo, I hit upon a novel idea: a poem to honor President Barack Obama. It would be a collaborative poem written by a diverse cross-section of American poets. Taking inspiration from two projects in which I had participated, *Starting Today: 100 Poems for Obama's First 100 Days* edited by Rachel Zucker and Arielle Greenberg and *Crossing State Lines: An American Renga* by Bob Holman and Carol Muske-Dukes, I conceptualized a project in which poets, reflecting Obama's historic legacy, would pass lines to one another. The renga, an ancient Japanese form of collaborative writing composed of two stanzas—a haiku and a waki—struck me as the perfect vehicle for this undertaking because it invites conversation. Two poets would each be assigned one stanza (haiku or waki), and their collaboration would be passed to two more poets, creating a chain of imaginative reflection on the legacy of America's first black president. The renga, as it emerged, would be published daily for 100 days at *Harvard Review Online*.

I wrote an invitational email to poets I admired and found inspirational, but also to younger poets whose intelligence and emotional clarity seemed to me to announce a new energy in American poetry. Within hours of the first round of invitations over a hundred poets had committed to participate, and by the end of the day nearly 200 hundred had signed on to this literary undertaking. One activist-poet declined to participate on the grounds that she could not support a president who had sanctioned drone warfare, expressing dismay at what she viewed as a contradiction in such an otherwise humane person. Another, who initially accepted the challenge, respectfully withdrew from the project for similar reasons.

Over the course of a week, I worked out the pairings. This was an arduous process in itself, as I wanted poets who would not create an echo chamber but generate productive tension either in style or thematic approach. My only instruction to participants was to keep the poem in the spirit of celebration. *Harvard Review* editors Christina Thompson and Chloe Garcia Roberts and I all agreed early on not to let the poem become overwhelmed by the climate of political rancor that seemed increasingly to define public life after the election. We wanted the project to retain its sanctity as a commemorative poem rather than a literary work of protest, leaving to others the articulation of outrage.

Former poet laureate Robert Pinsky opens *Renga for Obama* with Carol Muske-Dukes, who together set the tone of the project: "Island-born, cool lava-bloom. / You. Presiding, laurel-crowned." What follows is an opulent act of imaginative power that, as I wrote in my remarks at the outset of the project, "expresses the profound sense of gratitude we have for a modern political leader who is measured, thoughtful, humane, and literary-minded."

But gratitude is not the only note that finds expression in this poem. Many of these collaborative stanzas give a nod to Obama's sense of style, "his cool." Others implore him to remain active in political life, alluding to some of his legislative victories:

who touches this book—
I, too, sing America—
keep on keeping on

•

how many able to breathe
thanks, ACA   That's just math

My favorite however are the stanzas that praise First Lady Michelle Obama for her elegance and leadership. (A small but illuminating fact: her name appears more frequently in the poem than his.)

And because protest in America cannot be policed, poets also give voice to a fear that the incoming administration will follow through on its promise to undo social programs that dignify and uplift American lives — abolishing public healthcare, defunding the arts, raiding our national lands, building a wall. For many of the contributing poets, Obama's example is a call to continue the fight for what is right and best for the country:

> When you inspired you
> did not forget the air re-
> quired to continue.
>
> •
>
> Did not forget the air, no
> more water: the fire next time.

What is also evident in reading the poem is the range of seriousness and humor with which each collaborative team went about their task. The rhetorical diversity and richness of language ("Be brown. Be Black. / Bewilder. Be wild. Be prez. / Be that that's been that") hints at the durability of the renga project. That humorous lines — "What big ears you have, / Mr. President! and heart / Big as big can be" — can coexist alongside more serious reflections — "What's more complex than / a body's continental /

history shining // past the old America / which is never past itself"—is a testament to the poem's ability to encompass all manner of playfulness and solemnity.

A word on how to enjoy this poem. *Renga for Obama*, like traditional Japanese poetry, invites contemplation. Each link insinuates and points to *what is not said* as much as to *what is said*, and, thus, the poem requires readers to meditate on the collaborating poets' words. For this reason, I recommend reading a few stanzas at a time. What might on the surface be inscrutable initially will open up possibilities of meaning, and you'll begin to notice patterns and echoes essential to the poem's structure and aesthetic harmony. The poets here come from all walks of life and are representative of our country. The act of listening to the different voices that make up our democracy is replicated in the act of reading this poem. The poem is fluid and unpredictable; its message to President Barack Obama is singular: *thank you*.

—Major Jackson

RENGA *for* OBAMA

Healing in winter
Lava-flower tea—its wood
Endures like laurel.

•

Island-born, cool lava-bloom.
You. Presiding, laurel-crowned.

a helicopter
lifts from winter lawns — yet your
verdant hope keeps on

•

the snow conceals a future
hatch of shadow dragonflies

The moon hidden there
In the folds of day, the gray
What blind bold walking

•

Sane voice burnt in black wax won't swerve
All I hope for now is reverb

Your weather said cool.
Cigarettes, oratory.
Who dubbed them mom jeans?

·

The moon doesn't care, I know.
Your light glows from the inside.

I wear black today
and step into mid-winter
solidarity

•

A gold breeze touches my work
shirt open to some sweet song

Old school. So cool, you.
Solitary writer dreams
Midnight floating world.

•

Sing Al Green to me, baby.
Sing Barack, sir, as you please.

Nobody said fuck
you like he did—a razor
nick quick as his smile

•

Romantic, dialectic—
yet a middle finger too.

Somebody said Yes
& the blood said Here We Are:
American Song.

•

And the bones too. The organs
and brain singing oh come back.

A country embraces
absence like something it's earned—
the gnarled math of dust.

•

You tried to legalize us,
brief hope. No, no se pudo.

Stand tall as a fir
as their axes scrape the bark
of sixteen seasons

•

new moon drones in borrowed light
trans abolition everywhere

Here in our thawed brook
calm floats one brown leaf despite
vile loud counter-song.

•

Beneath it, water deepens:
the ocean's voices lifting.

Amazing his grace
Note sermon, her garden
Our house built by slaves

•

What has flowered here
And not what follows

Made in Hawaii,
Jakarta. African cool.
And then came Michelle.

•

A garden kept them grounded.
Those two girls. Kale. Kohlrabi.

Here the fallen seeds
push up through the sprouting scrub,
scourge the noxious weeds.

•

Shook one's leaves ante up'ed fête
make 'em say, you. will. miss. me.

What big ears you have,
Mr. President! and heart
Big as big can be,

•

Big as the Pyramid & Sphinx
In the drifting sands of Time

My Southie mother
would have loved you the way she
crushed on Kennedy

•

Crushed like blossoms — rose attar
Brushstroke ideogram: you

Eight years sleeping through the night:
always the given
eight years in reprieve.

•

The rat sneaking through the weeds
rouses the owl, which takes flight.

I know I'm alive
for, even through this smoke, I
can still see your face,

•

your calmness a lei's fragrant
promise the string will not break.

scant ration of hope,
sustenance — a smiley face
of seven almonds

•

freedom branches one 2 3
storm light to come & to go

working the sown "and"
dowsing roots from glitter soil
our global bodies

•

part ether, part earth: gestures
test our being together

Waves don't stop talking.
Where is your voice guiding us
through rocky weather?

•

Without you the country spins
like a mad compass needle.

Ledbetter, S-CHIP; GIT-
MO slated, almost, to go;
Rose Garden signings.

•

A child's still, clear eye now wet
For the humble heart that cared

Now where is your voice?
The after: this hushed city —
rain lashing windows

●

Storm then come time does
Know my heart will tell

Snow falls on the path
where inalienable trees
like truth do not bend

•

sentinels at attention:
watchman's duty never ends.

We can. We will. Yes.
From marrow to groove. Yes. We
dare burden to break—

•

to carry our massive us.
Marching poets. Each. Beat. Leaps

Unafraid to cry
even at the podium,
steelheads under ice.

•

Such strict poise: only a knack
for joy scores your brow just so.

Lunar eclipse—we
Keep remembering your smile
In our firmament

•

Or now a plate you can eat
your warmed waffle off in peace

beach marriage queer grace
cancer free o-surgery
dear life! we praise you

•

we make the stars ours again
one by   one by   one by   ten

Palmyra destroyed,
I couldn't talk a whole day.
Frond-slaps in dry wind.

•

Switchblade Trump messing with us.
Please come back when you are strong.

Birds, elephants, whales,
us: all go along to show
glory; Obama

•

slips to the years ahead this
splendor-space, a realm: Bears Ears.

But his gaze and hers
held a beam of light steady
erotic, equal:

●

We applaud deep roots, the willow
dances the storm in wild resistance.

who touches this book—
I, too, sing America—
keep on keeping on

•

how many able to breathe
thanks, ACA   That's just math

Plumeria blooms—
fragrant islands on a tree
rise from common ground.

•

Over roots, over water
each passing step firms the earth.

What's more complex than
a body's continental
history shining

•

past the old America
which is never past itself

We … We … We … We … We …
The collective noun for all.
We ends and begins.

•

Cherry blossoms. One river.
Flowers ridden through DC.

Watch him see Michelle:
this is what a feminist
looks like, loves like, now.

•

Pomegranate, spikenard, phlox:
that garden's a promise, kept.

Look how we wave still,
our bodies one glowing beast
united in grief

•

our linked arms raised, your steadfast
millions churning the bright air.

Tended. Intended.
Care like fingers stripping vines
from the stalk. Sugar

•

dissolves in our tea, now in-
visible, now everywhere.

Sho. Be brown. Be Black.
Bewilder. Be wild. Be prez.
Be that that's been that.

•

Pull dignity off yo' rack.
Strut that hazelnut strut, Black.

Black beyond moonlight
Man alone before nations
Hail the chief once more

●

Othello, Othello not
we, the many Iagos

Blue parks, Greenland sharks
Louisiana black bear
Brown out the mean time

•

The feral silence of earth,
breath held for millennia.

Water, seasons, heart.
You move like the sea's measure—
dropping the mic cool.

•

Pinned to my memory: petals of light.
Anxiety, scatter, seagull the sky.

Barack and Michelle
if we sing in this dark wood
would you reappear

•

pragmatist-preacher & cool
in the grass all I got this.

Keys given over
in such difficult weather—
his coat braced snowfall.

•

Pikake flowers bloom here,
this season come too early.

reverse \ // re-
spite /// then \\ PLUNGED {into} the (:::) fi-
re this* [time]: ? /¡ (#HurtBad)

•

Trans. Abs. Ne-d. n▪wh▪▪▪ Alt.(music)
These Floaters remain ~~{gáem³ }~~ glass state

Even my far sea
ferried your voice, which buoyed us,
black bellyfuls, hope

•

All empires end; we're empire
Now. New song: disturb the peace.

Song in Barry-key:
Be love and light of brisk waves
Of we are, we hold

●

to be self/selves evident
in light, in darkness: beauty

When you inspired you
did not forget the air re-
quired to continue.

·

Did not forget the air, no
more water: the fire next time.

Dave Chappelle marveled
at a black White House party —
(With Bradley Cooper).

•

Is it now too late to make
America hip again?

To thrust spangled fist
up, splintering sky, shattering
blue? And finding you?

•

Barack, a word that means blessed.
Obama, from obam: to bend.

your head gone to gray—
the winter weight of knowing
and knowing better

•

oceanic what was lost
ice cannot hold back the sea

Bloom spark spits its seed
into the nation's soil.
A vision sows fire.

•

To our children you will be
both past and future: a seed.

After long winters
53rd Street sprouts where you
walked, read, loved Michelle.

•

New blooms in Belfast, in Paris:
the globe turns, still missing you.

Blessings, oh Singer,
lilies, flags, oh church, Amens!
Grace, valor, sun's burst

•

brings us into the streets. Your
voice and our grief lead us home.

You smiled and lit up
the White House, made it rainbow
because love is love.

●

That amazing grace you had
in Charleston SC to sing.

At home body surfing
In those violent blue waters—
Clear pupils of the law

•

Look up! The nebula
exalts a quieter sky.

The moon holds the hand
of the dark, a child afraid
to lose her mother:

●

O's hand touched black child's cheek. Now
ICE rips Mamá's hand from mine.

I hold the gold lei
Thank you for holding us toward
a realized élan

•

Thank you in peace, in pieces
Of torn petals, lean back black

The window is cracked.
A blizzard is arriving.
Your clear, distinct mind

●

a ray of sun in gray sky
melting the Chicago cold.

Such was the dignity
you gave us now we can only
weep for its absence:

•

after the horn's supreme note,
a hush gathers, deepens, brims.

Your haiku's long song
Our clouds blooming ceaselessly
All luminescence

•

your hand in Michelle's high-raised
you rescued the gouged nation

Born in the twenty-
aughts, we watched you model grace.
And soon we will vote.

•

Come back, young South Side lovers
who read Gandhi: rule again.

Hope relentlessly
storms ahead. Ascendant wind
howls its will: Soon. Still.

•

Dark the dark night. We mothers
Sing our various blossoms.

Spaces between trees—
silences you searched for words
that fit the country.

•

Jigsaw moon of the tropics
where fugitive tongues crackle.

Sawgrass sounds. The moon
over Bears Ears, Flint spillway,
arctic birds blown south.

•

Inside the buds, new leaves wake.
Inside us, your strength unfolds.

affordable walls
delivered by droves across
borders without care

•

each blood boned body cracked the
house, white; gulp blue skies 'til red

White ripple Blue moon
Black boy stirs the pond's cool face
Water remembers

•

pulled cig and head ungrayed. How
laughter churched us then. And now?

Picket signs, spring
Some knowledge, supposed to stay
Encoded in smile

•

Come, rain. Your floods, your thunder.
You can't halt these seeds from bloom.

Trillions of stars. Ours.
Above, Orion's hunger.
Low, roots grow like hands.

•

Sixty more harvests, as the
soil goes now. Then ours no more.

From the great droop'd star
drifts the black bird's rapt carol.
How do I live now?

•

It has never been more clear
Thank you water, sun, Karl Marx

Bullets speak ill riffs
in dreams. One hundred ravens
lift Black President

•

De verdad, spending mad hope
South Side swagger in effect

That deep, quiet voice.
Deep, quiet, ferocious voice
sings. Amazing grace.

•

Our children's children's children
(sweet that sound) speaking of you.

Self-fulfilled, the sun
stands on the shoulders of the
dead — who sang, who sing

•

as they melt the snow around
their stones shining as the sun

Mourning doves hue &
cry as one branch falls after
another near miss

•

Obama, grave consoler,
once soothed our mutual grief

The water is gone—
lines like eyelids on concrete
faces of buildings

•

& beneath the moon: a hoop,
left hand high, windblown strings.

Blue herons persist
in riparian thickets
along Potomac

•

We needed a sugar snow
a tongue-break in sleep season

The court's empty now,
    no one around for pick-up.
        Scoop shot kiss off glass—

•

Ricocheting history.
History the ricochet.

Red sand under snow:
wild lands sigh to the civil,
inviolate sky.

•

There the hive hangs undefiled;
honey brims the cells within.

So morning's first call
quickens even spring-cold limbs
with contagious song!

•

Through evening's floating gold.
I am listening to you.

In the lion's skin
the beginning of something
none of us had seen

•

out of the strong something sweet;
a bright sun casting shadows.

—then suddenness: wing
of yellow, cracking the glass,
when the whole pane bursts:

●

the sound of bright shards scattered
over the floor like sunlight.

In the snow-melted
slush, a nested sun sets. You
knew how to spin thread.

●

How to slow dance, twirl Michelle.
O sweet nostalgia "At Last."

A gray day, a cold
room, a memory of the
island while walking

•

two times round, half a child's life,
the land must heave its heart back.

What tastes bittersweet
is still sweet; in daybreak pink
Americans waltz—

•

a chandelier of starlings
tangled in each other's songs.

Round the paddock too,
a new lob-ear breed gallops,
heedless of horse graves.

•

Whatso goes leans to sex from
me; I drink the Euphrates.

The thorns too are bright.
In the sick ward a girl counts
ways the light can break—

•

a reminding: with steady
rain even the mountains kneel.

That threshold we'd crossed—
have we crossed back—history's
Jubilee—and Knell—?

•

Don't ask, don't tell? You said NO!
All souls finally equal? Shout! Ask! Tell!

Winter all this spring—
crepe-paper blossoms wither
in cruel weather.

•

Stormsnowwindheatdroughtfloodscold—
Checks and balances can't hold.

To be straight, fall trees
bend in the wind. The pond seeks
light in the near-dark.

•

How hurt blesses the branches,
how dawn brings them into bloom.

A tree or a stand
—air, house, breath—windward unbuilt
lightless bright unfurled

•

Breath in a reflecting pool—
the turn of an even sky.

And yet, it hasn't
blossomed yet: the emoji
for "Barack come back!"

•

We are waiting — hands on hearts,
basketballs crooked, ball shoes laced

Capacious smarts; stark
redress of grievances. Bare
limbs break then bloom: stars

•

undress; glow of open palms;
long overdue hope, start, psalm.

Heal these thick blood-fields
where no apology grows —
Breakfast. Lunch. Dinner.

•

Around a widened table,
Feast. On change. Savor honor.

To run into spring—
what goes up must then come down
Like weather, ethics—

•

Someone's going to catch the
damn ball, throw it high again

go high when discourse/
spirals downward to undermine/
winds of chance and change

•

twine together vast, grim storm
the oak, spruce, magnolia, palm

Bears Ears, Katahdin, now saved
Papahānaumo-
kuākea, Sand to Snow

•

Ellis Island rain, inside
my pocket, third class steerage

Sakura on campus
at full volume:
haven't they learned anything?

•

In gaslight pink petals sift,
drift. Hard fruit will come of this.

Frail cherry blossoms
Hit by freak springtime snowfall
Still singing. Come sun.

•

Agitation of petals,
Worms churning beneath wet grass.

What may this old form
spread out like clover over
the nation impart?

•

The eyes of the long-gone past
Will always remain open

The bee-loud linden
blooms — bright yellow elegies
against extinction.

•

How to mitigate collapse:
open a nation's garden.

By motorbike, spring
markets blur—you drive into
green islands of sound

•

Sheltered monk seal, black coral,
seamounts: ocean monuments

To share an island.
And (floating) roots. A ticket.
Water's syllables.

●

Glitter path on homesick pond.
Spring frost. Moonlit consciousness.

Mean River rising,
and you standing like the tree
      beside the water ...

•

Crucial purposes fulfilled:
no fear of beauty, of truth.

sea black/sea(l) light: we
turn to what (we) hope won't bleed:
hear (me): see: be(lieve):

•

Learned to wangle a deathly
system. No Monet fuzz there.

Oh, April, what lies
this full moon passes over,
what cross purposes.

•

The moon itself cannot lie
but dumbly sings only, "Moon."

emerging maple
leaves and their bright red seed-wings
sail into spring seas

•

Calf nurses beneath pink moon
while fitful geese carve the sky.

Around the White House
Gold light forever shines on
With your memory

●

Illumines late-season thanks:
bloom bitten by frost's surprise.

Long for that lucid
inch of tide to gloss again
the harlequin stones

•

Let rivers gleam into seas
to rise closer to the sun

Weddings on the moon
All the vows were drifting glass
Now we stand on earth

•

Obergefell v. Hodges
Our lace tessellate endures

The frozen swell: heart
gap, sun-locked wall of boulders
makes no neighbor good.

•

The sharpest winter shadows
Slip off into fogs of spring.

Hawk wing span open
White House windows know Black free.
Rainfall sudden light.

•

Open, yes, hawk or flower.
Above him, the leaves applaud.

You opened both hands,
let ours go: we hurtle back,
reach for each other—

•

each rearranged into ache.
Ache springing into action.

Altitude. Your words
soaring over winter fields.
Contrails in dark sky.

•

Below, blue lambos reflect
hope: bringing us back to light.

When you pause, the world
waits, breathing in while the trees
breathe out, Obama

•

now, we want your language back
is it where you are: in us?

don't mow your lawn, wild
flowers will grow. but that's if
you have a lawn. who

•

siphons sun grass silt/hugs seed?
do-good kernels power bleed.

Once in a country,
song that feathered, bright anthem:
Aretha, do right.

•

Cold morning, hope's counterpoint.
Michelle's coat, too light, tied closed.

Winter won't relent,
won't release the language trapped—
torn page under ice

•

wind carries rebuttal blues
to Spring's visionary eardrums

After eight years
of love, burden, spring blooms tender
earned, radiant peace.

•

Break the state of ever-war,
dark birthstone, the heart's carnage.

You perfectly fit
the house that stood for a time-
less sense of purpose

•

Someone's swiped the welcome mat
wiped their wee hand on the drapes

Our president   gone
Grief   shall not be   our master
3 million   march   strong

•

Witty. Compassionate. Strong.
Adjectives line up, march on.

My trombone hits G
above the staff: regal tone
sings like memory . . .

•

nothing has touched me like this,
like this, since last December.

How many boys now
bear your name, your global sons
coming up hard, fast

•

New sounds enter our story
Teach us to hear other ways

As Rome's calendars
began in March: Obama,
we started with you.

•

But oppose the Muslim ban.
Donald Trump: very bad man.

blue for renegade
for fragility and luck
& for one who is blessed

•

by better skies, brightening.
Bending arc of history.

Who said a night sky
Only appears black then made
Bombs burst them blacker?

•

No broom fit for ash from war,
Or hair from fades and presses.

Wings gliding at dusk
One book inside another
Night fills emptied shelves

•

In the ditch, water flowing—
Now an eagle feather wind

Four bright bits of blue
tape mark where the poster hung
in the bathroom stall.

•

The ghost of old sentiment
vibrates cyan and urgent.

You stormed. You shone. Black
President a rainbow in
A sky of unknowns.

•

A letter. New teeth. Cold milk.
Hot blue inksong, chalk dust beam.

I remember the river
Potomac and the canoes
Of slavers paddling south.

•

Heart of the breath wakes up on
a bench, feels fairly far out.

unmeasurable
love changing hands 2 fists bump
both so beautiful

∙

Your question — your answer. O
what does it know? fistinsnow

Oh Kalaupapa's leper's friend.
Their stone of love, hand-painted:
No blame. No shame.

•

I'll say it, no shame, I miss
your shine, abhor this winter.

Anything that crosses costs
someone. Tree or bench
or boat: you held them all

•

O,,, where fernfrond touches ground,,,
fire sparks — burns, O,,, slow vow,,,

Philadelphia
Your halfness, mine, became ours.
Spring: Nothing, then green.

•

Fall: A plague of white, white
Preening cuckold of our land.

One—: grin's brim-charged—: bow
Quivers—: deep :—the tongue-struck—:
dark—: prescinding white noise

•

Dark struck tongue, the deep quivers,
I can think of nothing else.

washington cobblestones
wet with rain remember
your footsteps

•

now we say aloha, say
harambee, We the People

CONTRIBUTORS

KELLI RUSSELL AGODON is the author of six books • KAVEH AKBAR's debut poetry collection is *Calling a Wolf a Wolf* • ELIZABETH ALEXANDER is a professor at Columbia University • PAMELA ALEXANDER is the author of *Slow Fire* • EVE ALEXANDRA is the author of *The Drowned Girl* • KAZIM ALI is the author of *The Far Mosque* • CRISTIN O'KEEFE APTOWICZ is the author of *How to Love the Empty Air* • DERRICK AUSTIN is the author of *Trouble the Water* • A. H. JERRIOD AVANT is the recipient of two fellowships from the Fine Arts Work Center in Provincetown • DAVID BAKER's latest book of poems is *Scavenger Loop* • PETER BALAKIAN is the author of seven books of poems • SALLY BALL's most recent book is *Wreck Me* • MARY JO BANG is the author of seven collections of poems • J. MAE BARIZO is the author of *The Cumulus Effect* • CATHERINE BARNETT's *The Accursed Questions* is forthcoming • ALIKI BARNSTONE is the poet laureate of Missouri • SAMIYA BASHIR is the author of *Field Theories* • ELLEN BASS is the author of *Like a Beggar* • JAN BEATTY is the author of *Jackknife: New and Selected Poems*

- APRIL BERNARD's most recent book of poems is *Brawl & Jag*
- CHARLES BERNSTEIN's most recent book is *Pitch of Poetry*
- ANSELM BERRIGAN is the author of *Come in Alone* • LILLIAN-YVONNE BERTRAM is the author of *But a Storm Is Blowing from Paradise* • JEN BERVIN's latest book is *Silk Poems* • REGINALD DWAYNE BETTS is the author of *Bastards of the Reagan Era* • TARA BETTS is the author of *Break the Habit* • JILL BIALOSKY's new volume of poetry is *The Players* • MICHELLE BITTING is the author of *The Couple Who Fell to Earth* • SOPHIE CABOT BLACK's most recent book is *The Exchange* • NOAH BLAUSTEIN's *After Party* is forthcoming • MICHELLE BOISSEAU was awarded a 2017 fellowship from the Guggenheim Foundation • ROGER BONAIR-AGARD is the author of *Gully* • SUSAN BRIANTE is the author of *The Market Wonders* • JERICHO BROWN's second book won the Anisfield-Wolf Book Award • LEE ANN BROWN is the author of five books of poetry • JENNY BROWNE's most recent book is *Dear Stranger* • LAYNIE BROWNE's most recent collection of poems is *Practice* • MAHOGANY BROWNE's *Black Girl Magic* is forthcoming • STEPH BURT is the author of *Advice from the Lights* • GABRIELLE CALVOCORESSI is the author of *Rocket Fantastic* • MARILYN CHIN's most recent collection of poem is *Hard Love Province* • NAN COHEN's second poetry collection is *Unfinished City* • ALLISON ADELLE HEDGE COKE's books include *Rock, Ghost Willow, Deer* • HENRI COLE is as okay as possible post-

Obama • MARTHA COLLINS is the author of *Admit One: An American Scrapbook* • MARK CONWAY's *In the Middle Sky* is forthcoming • NICOLE COOLEY's *Of Marriage* is forthcoming • PETER COOLEY's tenth poetry book is *World Without Finishing* • EDUARDO C. CORRAL is the author of *Slow Lightning* • P. SCOTT CUNNINGHAM's *Ya Te Veo* is forthcoming • KRISTINA MARIE DARLING is the author of twenty-eight books • THULANI DAVIS is the author of *Playing the Changes* • ERICA DAWSON is the author of two collections of poetry • GREG DELANTY teaches at St. Michael's College, Vermont • ALISON HAWTHORNE DEMING is the author of *Stairway to Heaven* • MATTHEW DICKMAN's *Wonderland* is forthcoming • MICHAEL DICKMAN's most recent book is *Green Migraine* • KATY DIDDEN is the author of *The Glacier's Wake* • MAGGIE DIETZ is the author of *That Kind of Happy* • LATASHA N. NEVADA DIGGS is the author of *Twerk* • ALEX DIMITROV is the author of *Begging for It* • TIMOTHY DONNELLY is the author of *The Cloud Corporation* • GREGORY DONOVAN is the author of *Torn from the Sun* • MARK DOTY's most recent book is *Deep Lane* • DENISE DUHAMEL's most recent poetry publication is *Scald* • CAMILLE DUNGY is the author of *Trophic Cascade* • NICOLE TEREZ DUTTON is the poetry editor at the *Baffler* • CORNELIUS EADY is the co-founder of Cave Canem • ELAINE EQUI's most recent book is *Sentences and Rain* • ROBERT FARNSWORTH's most recent book is *Rumored Islands*

• Farnoosh Fathi is the author of *Great Guns* • Andrew Feld is the author of *Raptor* • Annie Finch is the author of *Spells: New and Selected Poems* • Adam Fitzgerald is the author of *George Washington* • Nick Flynn's *I Will Destroy You* is forthcoming • Charles Fort is the author of *Mrs. Belladonna's Supper Club Waltz* • Tonya M. Foster is the author of *A Swarm of Bees in High Court* • Vievee Francis is the author of *Forest Primeval* • Jonathan Galassi's most recent book of poems is *Left-handed* • Sarah Gambito is the author of *Loves You* • Chloe Garcia Roberts is the author of *The Reveal* • Danielle Legros Georges is the poet laureate of Boston • Carmen Giménez Smith is a poetry editor at the *Nation* • Jody Gladding wishes Barack Obama were still in the White House • Rigoberto González is a professor at Rutgers-Newark • Kathleen Graber is the author of *The Eternal City* • Jorie Graham is the author of thirteen collections • Arielle Greenberg's latest book is *Come Along with Me to the Pasture Now* • Linda Gregerson's most recent book is *Prodigal: New and Selected Poems* • Rachel Eliza Griffiths is the author of *Lighting the Shadow* • Jessica Hagerdorn is the author of *Dogeaters* • Kimiko Hahn is the author of *Brain Fever* • Alysia Nicole Harris is the author of *How Much We Must Have Looked Like Stars to Stars* • Francine J. Harris is the author of *Play Dead* • Matthea Harvey is the author of five books of poetry • Yona

Harvey is the author of *Hemming the Water* • Tom Healy was appointed to the Fulbright Scholarship Board by President Obama • Todd Hearon is the author of two collections of poetry • Jennifer Michael Hecht is a poet and historian • David Henderson's *Obama, Obama, Obama* is forthcoming • John Hennessy is the author of *Bridge and Tunnel* • Juan Felipe Herrera was the poet laureate of the United States in 2015–16 • Bob Hicok's *Hold* is forthcoming • Jane Hirshfield's *The Beauty* was long-listed for the National Book Award • Jen Hofer is a poet and translator • Bob Holman is the founder of the Bowery Poetry Club • Garrett Hongo was born in Volcano, Hawai'i • Erin Hoover is the author of *Barnburner* • Ailish Hopper is the author of *Dark-Sky Society* • Fanny Howe is the author of *The Needle's Eye* • Marie Howe is the author of *The Kingdom of Ordinary Time* • David Huddle teaches in the Rainier Writing Workshop • Maria Hummel is the author of *House and Fire* • Angela Jackson is the author of *It Seems Like a Mighty Long Time* • Didi Jackson's *The Killing Jar* is forthcoming • Gary Jackson is the author of *Missing You, Metropolis* • Major Jackson is the author of four collections of poetry • Kimberly Johnson is the author of *Uncommon Prayer* • Hettie Jones is a writer living in New York City • Patricia Spears Jones is the recipient of the 2017 Jackson Poetry Prize • A. Van Jordan has published four books of poetry • Lawrence

Joseph is the author of *So Where Are We?* • Fady Joudah is the author of *Footnotes in the Order of Disappearance* • Ilya Kaminsky's *Deaf Republic* is forthcoming • Kirun Kapur is the poetry editor of the *Drum* • Mary Karr's *Tropic of Squalor* is forthcoming • Julia Spicher Kasdorf's *Shale Play* is forthcoming • Vincent Katz is the editor of *Readings in Contemporary Poetry: An Anthology* • Donika Kelly is the author of *Bestiary* • Amy King is the author of *The Missing Museum* • Michael Klein's recent book is *When I Was a Twin* • Joanna Klink is the author of four books of poetry • Ruth Ellen Kocher is the author of seven books of poetry • Jennifer Kronovet is the author of *The Wug Test* • Keetje Kuipers is the author of two collections of poetry • Florence Ladd lives in Cambridge, Massachusetts, and Burgundy • Deborah Landau is the author of three collections of poetry • Quraysh Ali Lansana is co-editor of *The Whiskey of Our Discontent: Gwendolyn Brooks as Conscience and Change Agent* • Dorothea Lasky is the author of *Milk* • Rickey Laurentiis is the winner of the 2014 Cave Canem Poetry Prize • Dorianne Laux teaches at North Carolina State's MFA Program in Creative Writing • Sydney Lea is the author of *No Doubt the Nameless* • Katy Lederer's *The bright red horse— and the blue—* is forthcoming • Joseph O. Legaspi is the author of *Threshold* • Genine Lentine is the author of *Poses: An Essay Drawn from the Model* • Jan Heller Levi is the author of *Orphan* • DANA LEVIN's most recent book is *Banana Palace* • ADA LIMÓN is the author of *Bright Dead Things* • TAN LIN is the author of thirteen books • TIMOTHY LIU's latest book is *Kingdom Come: A Fantasia* • JANICE A. LOWE composes music-text hybrids • MARIE-ELIZABETH MALI is the author of *Steady, My Gaze* • MAURICE MANNING is the author of *One Man's Dark* • SALLY WEN MAO is the author of *Oculus* • FRED MARCHANT's latest book is *Said Not Said* • GARY MARGOLIS is the author of *Raking the Winter Leaves: New and Selected Poems* • DAVID TOMAS MARTINEZ's *Post Traumatic Hood Disorder* is forthcoming • CATE MARVIN's most recent book of poems is *Oracle* • DONNA MASINI's *4:30 Movie* is forthcoming • JOSEPH MASSEY is the author of four collections of poetry • ADRIAN MATEJKA is the Ruth Lilly Professor at Indiana University in Bloomington • AIREA D. MATTHEWS is the author of *Simulacra* • SEBASTIAN MATTHEWS's new collection of poems is *Beginner's Guide to a Head-on Collision* • FARID MATUK is the author of *The Real Horse* • GAIL MAZUR is the author of six books of poems • KERRIN MCCADDEN is the author of *Landscape with Plywood Silhouettes* • SHARA MCCALLUM is the author of *Madwoman* • JILL MCDONOUGH is the author of *Reaper* • MAUREEN MCLANE is the author of *Same Life: Poems* • WESLEY MCNAIR's ninth book of poetry is *The Unfastening* • ERIKA MEITNER is the author of four books of poems • SARAH MESSER is the author of four books • SARA

Michas-Martin is the author of *Gray Matter* • Leslie Adrienne Miller is the author of *Y* • Ange Mlinko is the author of *Distant Mandate* • Tomás Q. Morín is the author of *Patient Zero* • Sawnie Morris is the author of *Her, Infinite* • Paul Muldoon is the author of *Selected Poems 1968–2014* • Harryette Mullen is the author of several poetry collections • Carol Muske-Dukes is the poet laureate of California • Marilyn Nelson is a chancellor of the Academy of American Poets • Aimee Nezhukumatathil's *Oceanic* is forthcoming • Urayoán Noel is the author of *Buzzing Hemisphere/Rumor Hemisférico* • D. Nurkse's eleventh poetry collection is *Love in the Last Days* • Naomi Shihab Nye's most recent book is *Voices in the Air— Poems for Listeners* • Ed Ochester's most recent book is *Sugar Run Road* • Rebecca Okrent is the author of *Boys of My Youth* • January Gill O'Neil is the author of three poetry collections • Meghan O'Rourke is an essayist and poet • Ladan Osman is the author of *The Kitchen-Dweller's Testimony* • Kathleen Ossip is the author of three books of poems • Alicia Ostriker is the author of *Waiting for the Light* • Ron Padgett's *How Long* was a Pulitzer Prize finalist • Gregory Pardlo is the author of *Digest* • Linda Pastan's fifteenth book of poetry will be published in 2018 • Julie Ezelle Patton's work appears in *Best American Experimental Writing 2016* • Willie Perdomo is the author of *The Essential Hits of*

Shorty Bon Bon • KATIE PETERSON is the author of three collections of poetry • PATRICK PHILLIPS is the author of *Blood at the Root: A Racial Cleansing in America* • ROWAN RICARDO PHILLIPS' most recent book is *Heaven* • ROBERT PINSKY'S most recent book is *At the Foundling Hospital* • ROBERT POLITO is completing a book about Bob Dylan • MARIE PONSOT is the author of five collections of poetry • D. A. POWELL is the author of *Repast* • ELIZABETH POWELL is the author of *Willy Loman's Reckless Daughter: Living Truthfully Under Imaginary Circumstances* • DANIEL EVANS PRITCHARD is the editor of the *Critical Flame* • KEVIN PRUFER'S newest book is *How He Loved Them* • KHADIJAH QUEEN is the author of five books • DEAN RADER'S newest book is *Self-Portrait as Wikipedia Entry* • BARBARA RAS is the author of *The Last Skin* • VICTORIA REDEL is the author of three books of poetry and five books of fiction • PAISLEY REKDAL is the author of a book of essays and five books of poetry • KATRINA ROBERTS is the author of four books of poems • MATTHEW ROHRER is the author of nine books of poems • BRYNN SAITO is the author of *Power Made Us Swoon* • SONIA SANCHEZ has written over sixteen books of poetry and prose • ED SANDERS is an investigative poet and writer • JASON SCHNEIDERMAN is the author of *Primary Source* • LLOYD SCHWARTZ'S most recent book of poems is *Little Kisses* • NICOLE SEALEY is the author of *Ordinary Beast* • VIJAY SESHADRI is a winner of the Pulitzer Prize in Poetry • PRAGEETA SHARMA is a professor of English at the University of Montana • JULIE SHEEHAN directs the MFA program at Stony Brook Southampton • EVIE SHOCKLEY is the author of *Semiautomatic* • ANYA SILVER has published three books with Louisiana State University Press • TAIJE SILVERMAN's first collection is *Houses Are Fields* • SAFIYA SINCLAIR is the author of *Cannibal* • GIOVANNI SINGLETON is the author of *American Letters: works on paper* • JOHN SKOYLE's most recent book is *The Nut File* • TOM SLEIGH teaches at Hunter College • PATRICIA SMITH is a professor at the College of Staten Island • MONICA SOK is the author of *Year Zero* • SOPHIA STARMACK is the Fellowship Writing Coordinator at the Fine Arts Work Center in Provincetown • MELISSA STEIN is the author of *Rough Honey* • SUSAN STEWART's most recent book is *Cinder: New and Selected Poems* • MELISSA STUDDARD is the author of *I Ate the Cosmos for Breakfast* • ARTHUR SZE is the author of *Compass Rose* • AMBER TAMBLYN is an author, actress, and director • TESS TAYLOR is the author of *Work & Days* • CRAIG MORGAN TEICHER is the author of *The Trembling Answers* • JEFFREY THOMSON's most recent book is *The Belfast Notebooks: Poems and Prose* • EDWIN TORRES is the author of eight books of poetry • JENNIFER TSENG teaches poetry and fiction for 24PearlSt • BRIAN TURNER is the author of *My Life as a Foreign Country* • CHASE TWICHELL's *Things as It Is* is forthcoming • LYRAE VAN CLIEF-STEFANON is the author of *Open Interval* • OCEAN VUONG is the author of *Night Sky with Exit Wounds* • SIDNEY WADE is the author of *Bird Book* • JONI WALLACE is the author of *Kingdom Come Radio Show* • WENDY S. WALTERS is a founding director of Essay in Public: A Humanities Project • ANTHONY WALTON is the author of *Mississippi: An American Journey* • ROSANNA WARREN is the author of *Ghost in a Red Hat* • AFAA M. WEAVER is the author of *Spirit Boxing* • JONATHAN WEINERT is the author of *In the Mode of Disappearance* • DARA WIER's *In the Still of the Night* is forthcoming • SUSAN WHEELER is the author of *Meme* • KATHARINE WHITCOMB's most recent poetry collection is *The Daughter's Almanac* • DIANA WHITNEY's first book won the Rubery Book Award in poetry • BRUCE WILLARD is the author of *Holding Ground* • CRYSTAL WILLIAMS is the author of four books of poetry • ELIZABETH WILLIS's most recent book was a finalist for the Pulitzer Prize • DAVID WOJAHN's eighth collection is *World Tree* • REBECCA WOLFF is a poet and prose writer living in the Hudson Valley • MARK WUNDERLICH is the author of three books of poems • JOHN YAU's *Bijoux in the Dark* is forthcoming • MONICA YOUN is the author of *Blackacre* • JAVIER ZAMORA is the author of *Unaccompanied* • MATTHEW ZAPRUDER is an associate professor at Saint Mary's College of California • ANDREW ZAWACKI is the author of *Videotape* • RACHEL ZUCKER is the host of the podcast *Commonplace: Conversations (with Other Poets)*

ACKNOWLEDGMENTS

The Renga for Obama project would not have been possible without the generous assistance of Houghton Library and the editorial staff of *Harvard Review*: Christina Thompson, Chloe Garcia Roberts, Laura Healy, Cecilia Weddell, Christopher Alessandrini, and Rachel Silverstein. We would also like to extend our heartfelt thanks to the many poets who rose to the occasion, contributing their individual energy and talents to this collective endeavor.